THE GREEN CUP

The
Green
Cup

✻

V. P.
Loggins

Cider Press Review

San Diego

Cider Press Review
PO BOX 33384
San Diego, CA, USA
ciderpressreview.com

First edition
10 9 8 7 6 5 4 3 2 1 0

ISBN: 978-1930781504
Library of Congress Control Number: 2016958950

Cover photo *Akkadian Cylinder seal and modern impression: bull-
man combatting lion; nude hero combatting water buffalo; inscription.*
Gift of Nanette B. Kelekian, in memory of Charles Dikran and
Beatrice Kelekian, 1999. Image in the public domain, courtesy
The Metropolitan Museum of Art

Author photograph by Joe Heimbach

Cover and book design by Caron Andregg

About the Cider Press Review EDITORS' PRIZE:
The annual Cider Press Review Editors' Prize offers a $1,000
prize, publication, and 25 author's copies of a book-length
collection of poetry. For complete guidelines and information,
visit ciderpressreview.com/bookaward.

Printed in the United States of America at Bookmobile in
Minneapolis, MN USA.

To Josh, Gina, Hayes and Tagg,
and for Becky

ACKNOWLEDGMENTS

Grateful acknowledgments are due to the editors of the following where some of these poems, in slightly different form, first appeared:

Cider Press Review: "The Wall"
Crannog (Ireland): "Summertime"
Fjord's Review: "Math and Imagination"
Free State Review: "Keys" (published as "His Father's Keys")
Defined Providence: "My Father's Hands"
    (published as "Father's Hands")
The Healing Muse: "A Breath," "Men at Sixty," "Taking"
Main Street Rag: "The Green Cup"
Maryland Poetry Review: "The Apple," "Going to Sleep"
Memoir (and): "Magnifying Glass," "The Snake Pit"
Poet Lore: "Pumpkin"
Ruminate Magazine: "Overcoat"
Slipstream: "Doorkeeper"
Third Wednesday: "The Custodian," "Flat Screen TV," "Grotto," "Paris"

I would especially like to thank the editors of *Third Wednesday* for first printing the following poems in their Featured Poet section: "Gray Feather," "Mother's Day," "Perennials," 'Postscript," "Promise," "Rejection," "Relic," "Summer Ice," "Tomatoes." Thank you also to the editors for submitting "Perennials" for a Pushcart Prize.

My thanks to Jody Bolz, Thomas Heise, and Thomas Lux. When he, Thomas Lux, agreed to write a blurb for this book, he did so without hesitation. I did not know then of his illness. And so it is with deep gratitude and not a little sadness that I acknowledge his kindness and generosity.

I am grateful for the attention, assistance, and friendship of John Beckman and Michael Zito. Thanks also to Marcela Valdes and Emily Griffin for their support. My gratitude goes as well to Carol Colatrella of the Georgia Institute of Technology.

Caron Andregg and Ruth Foley of *Cider Press Review* deserve my particular thanks.

And finally, to Steven Craig, whose steadfast friendship, faith, and encouragement have been fortifying, my profound gratitude. And to Becky, who reads everything.

*"And bring away this beautiful green cup with you," she said . . .
"And do not let it out of your hand . . . for at whatever time it will
escape from you, your death will not be far away."*

—Lady Gregory

This whole city is a grave.

—Natasha Trethewey

*The lamentable change is from the best,
The worst returns to laughter.*

—King Lear

Contents

PART 3

OVERCOAT

The sun rises, opening a red vein
across the bay. A cormorant sits
in the broken orange light.

As the sun shifts, it disappears
into a continent of clouds
that hovers in the morning sky

above the shaking water. But
in the space between the bay
and the clouds the sun wore

the splendor of its making
all over again. Like the coat
my father used to wear

on early morning walks
beside the lake. Now I
wear his coat, making myself

all over again, shaped into
a figure beside the red water,
watching the sun rise, the green

coat over my shoulders, hearing
each step confirm my place
where earth has felt this wound.

PART 1

On that green evening when our death begins,
Just what it was, is hardly satisfying . . .

—Philip Larkin

THE SNAKE PIT

The fantastic lived in those days.
We drove the long road south
through fog so thick at night the red
tail lights ahead of us were all we saw,
the bright, then fitful failings
of their burning eyes, my mother
admonishing my father to be careful:
Don't ride too close. And his retort,
Christ, I can't begin to see.

                      The dawn
would rise and fog would lift and we
would view the wooded mountains,
the cloudy valleys below us, and all
the blue light, it seemed, the world
could then contain.

                  Once we stopped
at a roadside shack, a lonely frame
of paintless wood adorned with signs
like dragons' scales announcing
the mysteries within: *Petrified Wood,*
Tiny Alligators, Shrunken Heads,
Coca-Cola (Midsummer Magic),
The Snake Pit—

                Which was sunk
like a secret into the mountain earth
behind the building, where for a nickel
you could stand on the precarious edge
of the wondrous hole and watch
the captive serpents, and be yourself
captivated.

             The more so if you paid
a dollar to see a man descend into
the pit, defying death, and stand for all

the world there like Vitruvian man,
snakes adorning outstretched arms
like Christmas tinsel out of season.

Summer Ice

And the road lay hot ahead of us
that August when we went *home.*
Displaced by chance and choice,
we moved from the Deep South
to a place they called *necessity,*
Bethlehem Steel on the south side
of Chicago.
          My father and grandfather
burned in the waterfall of fire
like the glowing mill of Vulcan,
the gut of hell, smelling of sweat
and molten metal, but returned with
a Baby Ruth in a shirt pocket damp
with effort for my brother and me.
We knew the word *promise.*

So when August came around
we traveled to the South like believers
to the altar, driving the long journey
through the Smokey Mountains
in a Chevrolet, fighting the battle
of summer swelter with two blocks
of ice in a bucket behind the front seat—
which slowly melted along the road
as hot air from the open windows blew
furiously across them and brought

a chilling heat. My father and mother
sang hymns as if all of heaven
were at hand. The highway rose
and dipped and slipped behind,
but in the faultless sun before us
it wavered like the glint of water.

PUMPKIN

They said I was as small as a pumpkin
and called me by that name. Not,
I now admit, a happy title,
but when they needed someone

to be the batboy, they came to me.
My father played into his forties.
Each autumn, after summer season ended,
barnstorming Negro League teams

came rumbling through the city,
their cars, sometimes buses, filling up
the parking lot outside the stadium,
their voices, laughter, enlarging

the very air. Inside around the diamond,
the clock of balls on wooden bats,
the smell of leather oiled until
a blackness grew inside the palms

with a mystery reserved, it seemed,
for someone truly happy. My father,
I now remember, one day faced down
the legendary Satchel Paige, who stood

like an obelisk upon the mound
and threw with certainty his famous
hesitation pitch. Then I saw the ball
go sailing like a star out to the fence.

When my father came to third with
a pop-up slide, safe, Mr. Paige

with his finger pointed said,
Tell Pumpkin his dad can hit.

PRETTY BIRD

was a rainbow in a cage. Sometimes
she would set the parakeet free,
watch it soar about the house, land
on the brace of the lampshade,
the curtain rod, hang on the curtain.

And when she called it, *Pretty Bird,*
it flew, obediently as a schoolgirl,
and lit upon the reed of her finger
before she placed it back into the cage,
where it hopped happily, it seemed,

onto the slender wooden peg, having
traded a free afternoon about the house
for a lifetime confined inside a world
of golden wire bars and birdseed.
We knew when it died because a rose

grew overnight beneath the willow.
Afterward our grandmother, like
an obedient schoolgirl, poured
a pitcher of water there day after day.
Breezes swayed the sad green drape.

MOTHER'S DAY

On Sunday nights we'd tune in
to *The Ed Sullivan Show,* fixed

in our usual places, my father

in his chair, mother in hers,
my brother and me on the sofa.

The acts would appear, following

one another, each wryly introduced
by a suited Ed Sullivan, his face

long and friendly, his tie held neatly

with a silver bar clipped to his shirt.
Like us, sitting in the living room,

watching performances in black

and white on our flickering screen,
Topo Gigio, Herman's Hermits,

The Beatles, Supremes and Elvis,

a man balancing spinning plates
on sticks, as if assuring us that

the world could be controlled,

though riots filled the campuses
and Vietnam seemed uncontainable.

Once on Mother's Day, while

Mr. Sullivan and Topo Gigio
traded harmless jabs, my mother

disappeared. When she returned

she balanced a platter on one hand
with an oven-warm chocolate cake

perfectly sized for the four of us.

She served the slices round in order,
my father first, my brother then me.

Outside the world kept spinning.

MATH AND IMAGINATION

A strong imagination creates the event . . .
— Montaigne

Perhaps it was unusual, how the classroom
was always comforting, the way light
fell through the windows when my teacher
raised the sash, the air on May mornings
lifting the edges of the papers on my desk.
And my desk, which was mine — and that's
the point — as solid and smooth-topped
as slate, waiting for me each day to return
and glad to have my presence once again.

So on the day Mr. Scarce was teaching math
(he had drawn fractions on the blackboard
in the shapes of people, giving one-third,
for instance, two arms and a hat, one-eighth
a skirt around wide hips), I began to gaze
outside the window and to dream of being
in Mexico where, I had read, a boy could ride
a donkey from one coast to another, donning
a red and yellow poncho and green sombrero.

When I returned from my imaginary journey
Mr. Scarce was no longer on fractions and
had moved into history. The other children,
all seeming to know now more than I, were
hauling books like bricks out of their desks
and slamming open the pages. As I began
to get my text, the air seemed suddenly lighter
and, though a little perplexed, I knew where I
had been, where to go, and how to get there.

THE DRINK

I

The park had two entrances, *both*
alike in dignity, two brick pillars
on each side of the road, an arching
wrought iron sign soaring like a black
rainbow from one pillar to the other,
the name of the park spelled out,
like Dante's warning, above the street
that wound its serpentine way through
the center, the silky concrete ribbon
flowing freely as the days appeared to be
when I was a boy spending my time
on that road and at the pavilion where
for a quarter you could buy a *Suicide*
and drink the mixture like a potion.

II

My mother forbade me to go, saying
I couldn't have business there. But
on summer days when school was out
I'd naturally sneak away to find the park,
grabbing my bike for *a ride around the block*
until well out of sight where I turned
to speed my way, feet and legs pedaling
as fast as I could, up and down, the circles
of my tires humming, spokes disappearing
in a transparent flash. What drew me
was the wonder of oaks that rose
like enormous clouds shading forbidden
precincts, and the pavilion where girls
would congregate to buy the *Suicides*.

III

I was lost in the luxury of it all, sweet
smells of cotton candy, bubble gum,
red ropes of licorice, concoctions
my mother never heard of, and the girls
who stood around the corners in the sun,
their hair like dark waterfalls shining
with forbidden light, two by two,
and sometimes more, but always there,
in conversations I would never know.
Until one day when someone called
me over and I felt the taste of copper
rising in my mouth, fear growing like
a crazy row of blackberry bushes
along the edges of my shaded wood

IV

of shyness. So grounding my bike
I walked into an unknown space,
floating inside, the balloon of my being
lifted on a breeze I hadn't known before,
taking me on a fearsome flight to the sun.
I wished for the oaks to spread a shade
about me, to cover me in darkness
like the grass that hid beneath them.
But the quantum, *forbidden transition,*
the unexpected, unlikely occurrence
that she would call me, would know
my name and say it, naming me as I
seemed to emerge from a shadow
like a serpent feeling the spring sun

V

for the first time after winter. I must
have moved slowly. My right hand
trembling with a paper cup, the drink
glowing with the broken light where
crushed ice floated like the words
I wanted to say but couldn't. She
took three steps and met me, her hand
outstretched to take the cup. I watched
her drink the *Suicide*. Then walking
toward her friends, she looked back
at me and seemed to make her way
without her eyes. Which tossed me
like the oak trees in a storm, leaving
me hoping to be forever shaken.

TO THE BONE

He held the bike at the top
of the hill, its handlebars

like shining antlers, its seat
a small black boat, waiting

for the two of us to climb
onto its cradle and fly head-

long down the white lane,
crazy with the April air,

laughing through the terror,
as we dashed like fallen stars

into the future. When we hit
the wayward stone and slid

like two logs down the rapids,
me on the skateboard of his back,

and he taking the road's anger,
we tumbled to a stop, seeing

the ping-pong ball of his shoulder,
red and white, crusted with wet,

black dirt, the bone sticking
like a scrimshawed antler

from the tear in his T-shirt.
And the beauty of it was

that Dean, poor Dean,
lay laughing at the accident,

careless of the consequences,
while I climbed to my feet,

shaken to my unscratched bones,
looking for words to describe it.

HAIRCUT

The chair was far too big for me.
      Its brown leather seat, porcelain arms,
    its chrome pump handle refulgent

in Saturday morning's sunlight,
      the headrest a loaf of Wonder Bread
    I couldn't reach until they brought

the milk crate out and placed it on
      the cushion, lifting me to the height
    of a real man. My thin legs dangled

like twin anemic waterfalls
      across the front of the chair.
    What'll it be? he asked my father,

taking up the menacing shears. *Not*
      too much this time, was the answer.
    We're gonna let him grow for now.

Then wisps of hair began to fall,
      seesawing like a feathery cloud,
    lighting upon the barber's cape

across my lap, the shoop and snip
      of scissors (for which the word snick
    must have been invented) butterflying

about the hollows of my inner ear.

MILKMAN

Four A.M. came early but I was up and ready,
for in the chirping darkness he arrived
to take me with him on the milk truck,

a white van with tall open doors and high seats.
It was a struggle to climb into the cockpit,
stepping onto the crosshatched steel floor

and taking the balance rod like a staff
in my right hand to pull myself up.
But when I managed to mount the high chair

I was a prince dangling my feet from a tall throne.
We spent that summer morning on the streets,
first stopping at one and then another

of the waking homes—he, king of the milkmen,
delivering the goods to porches and stoops
all around the city, leaping, it seemed to me,

in and out of the door, while I watched
and the sun began to make a tardy rise.
As day progressed (the hours—nine, ten, eleven),

heat began to grow in spite of the outside breeze.
He told me then that I could retreat into the cooler
and that I was free to have all the chocolate milk

I could drink. It was there in the chilling darkness,
bouncing about in the back of the truck,
milk bottles ringing like chimes against each other,

I began to sense the presence of unseen things,
feeling my way around the cartons, the treasure
of chocolate milk indiscernible from the white.

BLACK IRIS

When we saw him he had a cold,
wiping his runny nose as he read
the poems & spoke apologetically
of his flagging health. But in spite
of his condition he held his place
like a black iris, dark eyes flashing
through the tears he dabbed away

with white cotton handkerchiefs
he plucked like words from one
pocket then another, spreading
his language griplessly across
the room, seeds sown in a garden
where, as he might say, a man
can be beaten until he rises.

Like my mother: telling stories
of dragging bags through the fields
of her youth, the cotton growing
heavier each time she stuffed the sack.
She sang while the sun burned —
the bag swelling, the need growing —
sang until the song displaced the pain.

Tomatoes

When you blanch one the skin
peels off pretty easily, the way
blisters, once they have risen,

will peel to expose the blush

of tender flesh, pale and raw
and redolent. Known also as
beefsteak, love apple, these,

a knot of cherry tomatoes,

were plump and round as marbles.
By tasting one I remembered
when, in the flush of boyhood,

someone poured scalding words

across me, naming just enough
of my faults to make me feel
their bite. I boiled alone then

in the cauldron of my bedroom

till my parents appeared insisting
that I tell what had happened,
and how my mother said, *Don't*

think about it. And my father said,

Screw 'em, boy. Toughen up. How
I blanched there in the darkness
while the other children played

outside in the crimson light

of the dying day, their voices
bubbling through the air around me,
tearing my skin away, leaving me

appalled and wondering how long

this shame would last. Then I saw
the peeled tomatoes and I knew.
How beautiful beneath the skin

they were and bitter on the tongue.

GRIEF

So it became a yearly Thanksgiving ritual,
packing Sue, the pointer, into the trunk
and heading out of town into the cornfields
where the yellow stalks were candle wicks
bent in the posture of prayer. Grandfather
would raise the lid and release the dog
who always circled our legs and would sniff
the ground, her breath ghosting into the air,
as my father slipped on his hunting jacket,
as tan as the fallen field of harvested corn.
Stay behind me, he would admonish. So I
would follow him down the rows, furrow
after cold furrow, the dust of snow blowing
like a dream mist, while I watched my dad
searching for the pheasant that ran and hid
until Sue, pointing, stiff tail extended, would
force the bird into the air and the big bangs
would echo, one following another in quick
succession, until the bird fell like Icarus
out of the sundrenched sky. Then Sue
would circle the corpse until my father
would pluck the bird from the frozen row
and slip it into the large pocket of his coat.
Only then, when death was certain, did he
let me come alongside him to see the colors
of this royal bird, its feathers flecked with gold,
its limp neck ringed with a white collar.
Then I would fall again behind him as we
walked in line down row after fallen row
till we had flushed the birds from the field.

PART 2

The pungent oranges and bright, green wings
Seem things in some procession of the dead . . .

—Wallace Stevens

DOORKEEPER

after Sappho

The doorkeeper's feet are seven armlengths long,
each arm is forty-five feet. When they found him

he was lying face down in the needles, the pines
having lost their leaves when the hurricane

blew little boats of children across the sky.
The women saw him first when they went to gather

truffles and found him instead. The first to see him
was Beth who saw the eggplant of his big toe

sticking through the underbrush, which was
rare because in a pine forest the underbrush

has trouble growing, lack of light, they tell us.
But we think it's their will not to grow because

any time something grows around here
it finds itself like the doorkeeper, face down

in needles, arms like the twisted branches
of the Wood, doors blown wide open

because no one is left to close them.
No one can hear the knocking at the gate.

MAGNIFYING GLASS

He was left with little more
than an old picture book: pictures
of the boys running endlessly up
a hill beside the lake; me in

a snowy field bearing the little badge
of a Valentine's card; my brother,
hair close-clipped to his head,
with a baseball glove and broken arm—

which he saw with a magnifying glass
that magnified what was already in
his mind, and always there, what was left

to him, remarking how we never sat
a solitary moment, but always ran
like fallen leaves across the grass.

My Father's Hands

His hand was bone then, sticks
for fingers, loose skin around
his knuckles. When he sat
he let the dry branch drop
beside the chair. He was
content on breathing. Watching

him sleep, I noted the blue
and narrow rivers of his veins,
the small cave of his mouth
where words like sparrows hid,
the still smooth flesh around

his temple. But most of all
I saw his hands, once plump
as peaches, baseball hard,
and gentle as a milkweed.
When they opened dust
flew out instead of seed.

KEYS

They clung like a clenched fist
from the peg on the handmade

    pine house he screwed to the end

of the cabinet above the kitchen
counter, where a crystal bowl

    of orange candy wedges lay

like invitations to indulge yourself.
The keys to doors and padlocks,

    those we knew about and those

that none of us imagined. Some
within easy access, the shed, say,

    or the front and back doors

of the house, the car that sat
in later years like him, undriven,

    though every morning he hosed

the pine needles off its roof
and threw a wet circle round

    the tires just in case he got a wish

to run the roads again, flashing
across the Alabama countryside,

his trunk filled with a boxed bounty

of moonshine and memory. When
the weight of going through his things

dropped upon us, the keys were the last

to be sorted out. We laid the jangle
on the counter and looked around

for doors to open, tumblers to turn.

Finally we stood with those for which
we had no answers, bewildered,

beside the bowl of orange wedges,

unable to unclench the fist.

Red Clay, White Sky

There in the red clay, beneath the oaks,
among the pines, and where the sky
sails marble clouds, where wind
has leaves go scraping one by one
across the red clay, my mother lies
in death as she had lain in life.

November breezes lift my hair
as I stand here watching what
the eyes can't see, the mind knows.

When I turn the world recoils.

In the distance off the hill
a hawk glides circles in the sky
as if nothing at all has happened.

THE APPLE

When I was a boy
my mother used to stand before
the vanity and spray her hair
heavy with the scent of perfume.

I'd watch her hold the atomizer
like an apple in her hand
and squeeze the little ball
until the air was thick with mist.

Down through the bedroom light
the mist would float like fireworks,
crystal with refraction,
gold and silver prisms from above.

And now I keep remembering.
It is as if some perfume lingers
with the atoms of my mind
where only molecules can matter.

Mother, in the orchard of the grave
that is the bedroom of our sleep,
could you squeeze again the ball
that bursts the air to apple juice?

PEACHES

Sometime during the final week
he asked me to close the curtain.
The room grew dim with the days

as each slow hour passed. Hoops
of time began to link us, circling
in swirls of light-starved air

as palpable as peaches. Which came
to mind in the ever-growing darkness.
I rested in the day we stopped to buy

the basket. How warm they were
in afternoon sun, the humble wooden
stand bearing the red and yellow

grace of its burdens. How the man
said, *Smell 'em.* And we raised them to
our noses, our Georgia-minded mother

most of all, who knew nothing so sweet
as a peach. We watched her breathe,
my brother and I, the soft fruit cupped

in the chalice of her hands. Like him,
striving to breathe the peach-sweet air,
which in truth I had imagined, as he

refused the hard indignity of light.

ANNIVERSARY

Nestled on the lotus of his pillow,
his head rolling   slightly   to the right,
the oval of his open mouth
a wordless

            O,

he took his last breath, his throat
       cupping
at the base.
           A year now—this hour,
this day.

We watched and waited then,
not knowing when his breath was spent,
fractured:
       Is it now?
            Will it come?
Like John Donne's virtuous man,
his strength   manifest   through silence.

Do not   he seemed to say   mourn
this morning   for me . . .

So we stood beside and saw the light
touch of his going,
          feeling
    the stream
on which this flower floated,
carrying him
         away from us
and into us at once.

PERENNIALS

The rows appeared with April, my father
turning the ground beside the house,
the sole garden in the neighborhood.
Like something conjured each year.
Rows emerging from earth as straight

as any line set down by an architect,
the little sails of seed packs sitting proudly
on their small masts at each end, naming
whatever was planted there, the rectangle
of the plot as certain as a gravesite. I

was the boy my father allowed to watch
as he drew each row with a hazel stick,
set the seed into the soil, cut and placed
potatoes into drills. *This is how you love it,*
he said, as he dropped each new seed

into divots marked by the end of the hazel.
Remembered now these many years on,
like a man bent over a garden plot,
his shoes accumulating crumbs of soil,
his hands smoothing out the broken earth.

GROTTO

She fished, made cornbread, poured
buttermilk over a glass brimming with
saltines as salt-ridden as her language.
Working the counter at the coffee shop,
she called herself a professional server.

When we sat down to table, she laid
fried chicken on a platter in the center,
green beans and potatoes in oval bowls,
set milk and sweet tea in glass pitchers
at opposite corners, sliced tomatoes
and fanned them out like a deck of cards
on a white plate
               for their *aesthetic contribution,*
she said, expecting us (two boys and our father)
to be happy to have what she had made.

But when her pain, unknown at first to us,
became unbearable she turned to pills,
naming them *cough drops of love, cough
drops of love,*
               the addiction growing
as the tide of her strength receded. Then
there was no more chicken, no more fish,
sweet tea or sliced tomatoes. We watched
as a seawall of pillows grew around her,
rising about her bed, the sides of a grotto
she erected for the darkness and for good.

TAKING

In both cases, the last breath was inhaled
not released, not a final exhalation like the end
of a storm. No. But the holding on to life,
as if the storm were worth it, the hope of hope
that lies in the expectation that the next tornado
will miss the house and only take the barn.

Each one took, in the conclusive sense of the word,
as if with both hands what the hands could never
really hold, the air that passes through the fingers,
not so much like water, but like time itself,
unseen, unfelt, unless you force yourself to feel.
For each the last breath would never be released.

Yet we are now expected to let go, to give
into the universe what the universe had given,
to say the end was well deserved, and peaceful,
and that with all we can remember of the life
we are content to see it off. While the rain
is pelting, the barn door swinging off its hinge.

RELIC

Suddenly he was there, placing
his tools in the garage, taking
over half the space like a platoon
of one sweeping in to occupy
a lost valley. He hung his hammers

and shears like antlers on the wall
and turned a wooden wheel into
a carousel of jars filled with tacks
screws and nails, setting up shop
as the neighborhood upholsterer.

Tall and lean, with elegant hands,
he carefully handled the fabrics,
measuring twice and cutting once,
with the grace of a dancer, smooth
strokes following a line only he

could possibly see. He stretched
the chair bottoms till they were
as smooth as a still pond, taut
with silk he unrolled from bolts
to stitch and tack to the frame.

So when his hands began to shake,
his cutting line askew, his shears
dropped, his hammer failing to strike
the tack—when this happened often—
no kind word could console him,

no boy like me could volunteer
the sort of help he needed. I

watched as every day he tried
to fit another chair with grace,
to bring an old thing back to use,

to conquer in his battle what most
he hunted for, and that was time.
When he died my father closed up
the shop and gave his shears
like consecrated bones to me.

Now he bends above the table
of memory where a bolt of fabric
is stretched, his hands moving
like a breeze over water, shears
along the invisible line, cutting.

A SECOND DEATH

After the first death, there is no other.
—Dylan Thomas

The bus pulls out, exhausting the afternoon
with black dust. I stand on the corner where
the stop stands, and watch it rumble off.

I'm beginning to feel this—the way the bus
disappears down the street, turning as the road
turns, its guttural engine a death grunt

fading into the air. As he is fading. I've been
hearing his voice, words leaping like squirrels
from winter's branch to the boughs of spring;

seeing his face, animated in the quickness
of his laughter and dulled by the slow cupping
of his final breath. I've been riding down

a street neither of us foresaw, remembering
morning's childhood agitations when, sleep
in my eyes, I woke to hear him in the kitchen

chanting, *Gather ye rosebuds* or *Get up, get up
for shame,* as he patted down little spheres
of biscuit dough for breakfast. To die once

is death enough, as Robert Graves remarked.
So now I press to hold the sight of him unable
to rise without my help—then unable to rise.

Memory's a rumble dissipating in a black smoke.
As ghostly as midmorning moons. Daylilies at dusk.

GRAY FEATHER

She lives now in the black
and white photographs of

my memory. Which are not
black and white at all but casts

of gray, though I know her hair
was a black swan, a crow's beak,

a raven's feathers, and she loved
to wear a poppy red sweater

shouldered like a shawl over her
sleeveless black dress. Sometimes

she wrapped a white apron around
her waist, its strings back-hanging

beneath a carefully drawn bow.
Her patent leather shoes flashed

with a searing white light. As
she lay in the dark of her bedroom

alone on a Saturday night, I could see
the orange flash of a cigarette

like a pinprick in the darkness
before all went black again. When

the Greeks named Mnemosyne,
goddess of memory, the mother of

the Muses, they knew the grief
that grows with time. Floating

in loneliness like a gray feather
on a breeze across my mind, she

drifts, rises, settles, rises again
on cold, invisible morning air.

FLAT SCREEN TV

Because he suffered
       from macular degeneration,
              curved objects were hard
to see. A player in his youth,

he often held a ball in hand,
       turning it between his thumb
              and fingers, remembering
the feeling of easy tension

in his legs, the way a ball
       well hit brought no sting,
              no feeling to his hands at all,
remembering how after sliding

he'd rise, time stopped, and brush
       his pants into dissipating clouds
              of sunny dust before play resumed,
and he would take again

his three-step cautionary lead
       of guarded expectations.
              When his eyes failed him
he saw things mainly in two

dimensions, a flat world
       off to the side of his field
              of vision, turning his head
to see what lay so obviously

before him. And this is why
	he bought the flat screen TV,
		replacing the old curvature
of glass tube. When the Braves

were home in Atlanta, he
	never missed a game, satisfied
		to view, though darkly, what
played out in front of him,

a loose leg thrown like a shawl
	over the arm of his favorite chair,
		happy with the skewed world.
Until the end when he said,

Take it home with you.
	Your vision might someday
		fail you too, and then
you will be able to see.

IMPERFECT GRACE

All things do change. But nothing, sure, doth perish.
—Ovid

Once admitted he was never to return,
so the hospital room became home,

the word defined not by place and use
but by acceptance. At first the welcome

window showed the outside world unchanged.
Birds in the leafy maples sang their songs.

The leaves themselves waved, he said,
like his mother so many years before

as he walked off to school. And as
days passed he settled into a childhood

of needs: *Get me a water. Hand me the book.*
Will you rub my feet? Close the window.

We watched as this season of demands
drifted across the sill of silence and out

a different window. As the end approached
I thought of ospreys gliding on thin air,

noticed the dust had settled on the top
of the table. Even words changed meaning,

death, for instance, not cessation but release.

A Breath

Sometimes the dead
go on living. Like
the sound mourning
doves make when

they take flight. I've
come upon them
in the shade, among
the ferns, where green

lies too deep for names,
and they have flown
fearsomely alive with
their wings whistling

out of the dark. No
windhover, sun-washed
and buoyed, circling on
an updraft of joy, but

a quickened necessity
to fly from one green
shade to another. This
too is a kind of death,

an act of loneliness,
remaining, once heard,
like the last breath cupping
before the flight has come.

THE WALL

They lie here side by side
in the long sleep, and I
wish I could set my ear
to the ground above them
and hear the night-talk,
those unintelligible words

I strained to hear when
as a boy I lay in bed
on the other side of the wall
and tried to sleep. I would
knock on the ground as once
I had tapped the wall's barrier

only to hear my father say,
Take it easy over there.
Then I would close my eyes
and, drifting off to sleep,
convince myself
that the darkness loves me.

WEEPING ANGEL

Raise your head, weeping angel,
though you weep we have today.
Stay your tears. This garden grows
though we, not you, will die. We know

you weep for us and we are grateful,
but no one need be sad. The well
has at its bottom many mirrors,
and when we have arrived there we

will find the tears you've shed. So weep
no more for you have cried enough.
We cannot wish our state undone.

Together in this garden we
have felt the fullness of our fall,
and looking down we've seen the sky.

PART 3

Spring water suddenly broadcasting
Through a green hazel its secret stations

—Seamus Heaney

Going to Sleep

With my son in my arms we walk
downstairs from room to room
and blow out each light successively.

He leans his little face forward
as if to kiss; he blows, and then
the light clicks off: *It's magic.*

We climb the dim stair of sleep;
quiet, he grips my shirt against a fall,
and looks upward to the well's end.

We settle ourselves in sheets,
cool and clean like water,
and fall quickly away to dream.

I think of the salmon in the streams,
fierce, instinctive, fighting the flow,
returning to the pools of birth;

I think of my son, a father,
with his son blowing out the lights
impassioned in his passing future;

and I think of my father with his son
laughing in the circle of his arms,
blowing out the evening lights.

There is a backward motion
while we are leaping to the future
that touches the fish and us.

It is like a spawning in the mind
that generates movement
and spreads time across to time.

It is a wave turned inward on itself
reaching a mysterious shore
and tipping an awesome darkness with white.

LINCOLN ELEMENTARY

we are the past
alive in its
truest telling
> —A. R. Ammons

Coming back to it now is like
an eerie half-remembered dream:
the big wide-eyed windows
replaced with opaque cataracts
of gray glass squares; the crimson
façade a crumble of brick and mortar,
so frail and mortal in appearance
it's like the mansion of the dead.

Yet this is where we went to school,
where we learned of Lincoln
and where we heard the news
of Kennedy's assassination; where
we lined along the sides of the gym,
counting down the opposite line
so as to be matched up rightly
with the Juliet of our interest.

This is where we first spoke of
The Beatles and where we dressed
with other boys for gym class,
some of us as open as a gate
while others like gates closed
and locked with embarrassment.
Do I have to dress and shower?
And this is where we got over

ourselves and sometimes into
ourselves, taking more seriously
the names that someone called us
than our real names. The yard,
now weed-riven and neglected,
is where we once played kickball
and traded jabs and bubblegum.
The riddle? *What runs on the road*

and carries it on its back? Unwrap
that one if you can, buddy boy.
And this is where we've come
to tell the stories of our childhoods
to our children, as if this history
truly was a fragmented dream,
as Romeo says of a lover's night,
too flattering-sweet to be substantial.

The Custodian

You saved them from the trash heap,
my father's, your grandfather's,

pile of leaves and papers he burned that day
in the backyard, smoke rising to apotheosize

whatever it contained. In this case
the baseball cards. Nineteen fifty-nine

Mickey Mantle, a '61 Roger Maris,
the year he hit sixty-one, undoped

and losing his hair, "Say Hey" Willie Mays
and all the rest. I remember each one

and the pictured poses, the bat swung
and held above the right shoulder,

the back knee bent almost to the earth,
the famous basket catch that caught

my imagination. Then I knew
it truly was a game, the one I saw

in black and white on the TV, the one
I played on the field in the echo of praise

I heard from my bleachered mother, ·
my father with us on the diamond's turf.

And you never told me that you saved them,
keeping the secret beneath your bed

in the old cosmetics case my mother,
your grandmother, used so long ago,

and where in the lightless silence lay
the mystery and holiness of memory

that you, the sole custodian, have now
revealed. How many are showing signs

of where I clipped them with a clothespin
to the front and back wheels of my bike?

REJECTION

He would say it to me from the third base
coach's box, which in truth he was standing

    outside of, as he clapped his hands together

before gliding his left hand, palm down,
toward the outfield, where with a certainty

    found only in faith, or maybe love, he was sure

I would spray the ball at the next opportunity,
not seeming to worry that I had already missed

    the first two pitches, taking a third for a ball,

low and outside, sure that the next pitch
would be within my wheelhouse. *Let's go,*

    it only takes one. When on the rare occasion

I actually did drop the ball into left field,
and the next batter grounded out, he would

    catch me as the inning ended and say it again:

See, it just takes one. And in point of fact it did.
How wholly American it all now seems to me,

    no matter that time and economy have changed

the nature of the game, have added, for instance,
the designated hitter and the relief pitcher

as standard players in the lineup, no matter

that the lyric bunt has virtually disappeared,
the homerun like an epic poem becoming

the mark of a great player. The belief

that all will be okay, no matter the opposition,
no matter the number of times that failure

like an old familiar returns to sport a sneer,

the words keep coming. He keeps standing
within my view, down the third base line,

one foot placed strategically outside the box.

SUMMERTIME

It is a July evening. The day
has been hot and repressively
humid. We have settled down
on your father's sofa, you
in your blue giraffe pajamas,
me with a whiskey in my hand,

when on the TV Kate Hepburn
in a wild flowered dress blooms
across the screen beside the canal
in Venice. She seems to capture
your attention and you nestle
into my side, watching, music

playing in the background behind
dialogue you cannot understand,
until she and Rossano Brazzi kiss.
Then you climb inches from my face,
eyes peering directly into mine.
A long second passes and I think

you want to say something about
what you have seen, but you seem
knowingly bewildered and silent,
as if words have not yet been invented
to describe what now is evident.
When you return to your place

beside me, you stab bare feet
into my ribs, roll and fall asleep.
I pull the blue giraffe pajamas across
your taut belly and carry you off
to bed. Outside the humid night
rattles with the songs of crickets.

MEN AT SIXTY

If Men at forty
Learn to close softly
The doors to rooms they will not be
Coming back to,

then men at sixty begin
to leave the doors ajar.
When they're looking
in the closet for a shirt

or in the kitchen
for a glass, they leave
the closet door,
the kitchen cabinets

open. Whenever men
at sixty are out
to the market, say,
or to the coffee shop,

sitting at the table
reading the *Times*,
they may glance up
to watch a person pass,

but no one looks at them
anymore; no one says,
What's the news? They
take their coffee black

and without sugar.
When they go to bed
they open the window
to the darkness.

THE GREEN CUP

I kneel to slip
the cup from the mud.
The river has receded
like a memory

and left the bank
revealed to reveal
the lost, perhaps forsaken
artifact

of the river's past.
I lay my finger round
and through
the empty ear

of its handle, hearing
the mud cheep,
feeling the ancient grip
of earth. What water

remains
seeps and fills the hollow.
Mud tugs against my tug.
The center holds

as if a sad
insatiable goddess
has pressed my heart
within her hands.

Paris

Just before I wake I am conscious
of the thought of the children at
the Luxembourg Gardens sailing
their little boats round the fountain

on a sunny day in April, the kind
of day you dream about when the air
is clear and the light is so transparent
that you are hardly aware of the pain

you experience in the ease of living.
And I can see the boys and girls
and their boats and I can hear
one child, a girl I think, asking

her mother in French if she can have
a drink, *Maman,* and her mother answering
in French, of course, *Oui, mon petit ange.*
And just before I wake I think

of just how lovely this would be if it
were not a dream and if I were really
there with these children and their little
boats sailing round the fountain as if

putting out to sea on some wholly new
adventure, the kind of thing that boys
and girls can do before they wake
as I am waking so far away from Paris.

GREAT CHANGE

The moon and Jupiter hang near
each other in the predawn sky
where the slow silver movement
of clouds gives the impression
that both Jupiter and the moon

are in motion, sliding westerly,
across the dark dome like some
heavenly migration where
the ancient gods have gone
and slowly disappeared, or like

a soul gravitating toward a body
or leaving one behind, or the first
Europeans whose ships brought
the new religion to the New World
then sailed back, their holds heavy

with the weight of gold. But here
embedded in the seeming motion
of these two bodies is the will
to hold themselves against the tug
of time, nature's proof that we

are not alone in our desire to freeze
the change, the great change,
best symbolized by the rising sun
making first the planet-star and then
the melting moon disappear.

Honor Flight

At the terminal a group of veterans,
some walking, some wheeled in chairs,
disembarked from the plane into
a flag-waving, hand-clapping crowd
awaiting them at the gate. And I

thought of you, reimagined you really,
here with your comrades, *teammates,*
you called them, wheeled or walking,
a smile bursting across your face
as bright as the glare that followed

your going. Now I am flying to see
your other son, my brother, who is
disappearing before our eyes. But let
this not be so final a loss. All things
can be reimagined, as now I see the two

of you playing catch beside the maples
you planted in the front yard of our house.

DRAGONFLY

The blue mountains and silver mist
is how I remember those return trips
to the place from which we came,
the place to which we yearly returned,
home, my parents called it, the point

of original departure, a lure to drag
us back. Blue mountains where trees
embraced the chilly hills with coats
of green fur and an insubstantial fog
that rolls now in memory's folds

of pitch and the dark ridges of time.
Where voices keep repeating like
Gregorian chants, over and over,
rituals of the past to be endured
as I ride the roller coaster highway,

up and down and up again, turning
as the road bends, skewered when
in the mind the car skips to a stop.
I'm a child, forlorn and excited,
in the backseat, hearing once again

the voices of my parents, embedded
in the car parked outside the house
above which a dragonfly cuts the air
with transparent wings and hovers
in a posture of expectation and light.

PROMISE

Neither of them could know,
one sitting before the rock face,

the other balanced on his thigh,
the one with his boater tilted back,

its rim like a halo around his head,
the other a child in a hat his mother

knitted for him. The one in a tie
and white shirt, the other a jumper,

both wearing their Sunday best
for the photo taken surely on

a Sunday morning in 1924 after
the church service, before retiring

to the house for a meal laid out—
fried chicken, green and navy beans,

cornbread, sweet tea and coffee—
by my grandmother. Neither of them

could know what lay before, Depression,
war, other children, the loss of a baby,

the death of a boy (my father's brother
not yet born), when this shot was taken.

But here it sits, framed in silver,
among the things on the nightstand

like a faint whisper, a promise kept.
They could not have known that I,

another son, these many years on,
would look upon this torn photograph,

their fading faces, as he wakes
to another morning, snaps on the light,

and finds the words to keep another kind
of promise that tears the heart open,

and remembers nothing but gold.

POSTSCRIPT

The path of white clouds
is like a wake on the blue
ocean of sky. As if something,
a boat, a whale, a dolphin,
has passed before and we
are watching all that remains.

I too remember how the fish
we caught and set into the bucket
sucked the air, its gills flashing
like an eyelid, how it flapped
in the bottom and struck
the galvanized silver sides

with its fins. This when I
was a boy and my father
took me fishing, where death
lay in our hands and life
tugged at the end of the line
disappearing beneath the black

silks of the rocking water.
I knew then that I should love
my life but all I wanted was
to change it—how the sun
seemed to change the sky
away from the heft of night

those early lakeside mornings,
the immensity of darkness
spreading before us like a sea

holding the mysterious bounty
my father then called *fish*. But
it wasn't until he began to gasp

the flaming air, hospitalized
and floating on the boat of his bed,
that I knew what kind of name
the word death was, what kind
of disturbance could leave a wake
across the teeming ocean above me,

what kind of love can make us
weep and, like our life, accept it.

NOTES

Epigraph: Lady Augusta Gregory. *Gods and Fighting Men,* 2nd ed. (Gerrards Cross, Buckinghamshire, England: Colin Smythe Ltd, 1970).

Epigraph: Natasha Trethewey. "Pilgrimage." *Native Guard* (New York: Houghton Mifflin Company, 2006).

Epigraph: William Shakespeare. *King Lear.* Edited by R. A. Foakes. Arden Shakespeare, 3rd ser. (London: Thomson Learning, 2006), 4.1.5-6. References are to act, scene, and lines.

Epigraph to Part 1: Philip Larkin. "Continuing to Live." *Collected Poems.* Edited by Anthony Thwaite (London: The Marvell Press and Faber and Faber, 1988).

The epigraph to "Math and Imagination" is from Montaigne's "Of the Power of the Imagination," which is found in *The Complete Essays of Montaigne.* Translated by Donald M. Frame (Stanford: Stanford University Press, 1968).

"Black Iris" refers to a poetry reading at Georgetown University by Yusef Komunyakaa and is dedicated to him. The line in my poem, "a man can be beaten / until he rises," refers to a line in his "The Cage, The Head," which is found in *The Chameleon Couch* (New York: Farrar, Straus and Giroux, 2011).

Epigraph to Part 2: Wallace Stevens. "Sunday Morning." *The Collected Poems of Wallace Stevens* (New York: Alfred A. Knopf, 1974).

The first line of "Doorkeeper" is based on Sappho's fragment 110, which is found in *If Not, Winter: Fragments of Sappho.* Translated by Anne Carson (New York: Vintage Books, 2002).

The epigraph to "A Second Death" is from Dylan Thomas' "A Refusal to Mourn the Death, By Fire, of a Child in London," which is found in *The Poems of Dylan Thomas.* Edited by Daniel Jones (New York: New Directions, 1971). The two poems quoted here are Robert Herrick's "To the Virgins, to make much of Time" and "Corinna's going a Maying," both of which may be found in many editions. For my purposes I have used *The Complete Poetry of Robert Herrick.* Edited by J. Max Patrick (New York: W. W. Norton, 1968). The reference to Robert Graves is from his "Leaving the Rest Unsaid," which may be found in *Collected Poems* (New York: Doubleday, 1961).

The epigraph to "Imperfect Grace" is from Ovid's *Metamorphoses,* bk. 15. Translated by Arthur Golding. Edited by Madeleine Forey (Baltimore: Johns

Hopkins University Press, 2001).

Epigraph to Part 3: Seamus Heaney, "The Diviner." *Death of a Naturalist* (London: Faber and Faber, 1991).

The epigraph to "Lincoln Elementary" is from A.R. Ammons' "History," which is found in *Diversifications* (New York: W. W. Norton & Company, Inc., 1975). Though I cannot document it, I seem to remember that the riddle mentioned in "Lincoln Elementary" is from Bazooka Bubble Gum's cartoon riddles of the 1960s.

The title of "Summertime" refers to *Summertime*, the 1955 Katherine Hepburn movie directed by David Lean and set in Venice.

The first stanza of "Men at Sixty" is borrowed from Donald Justice's "Men at Forty," which is found in *Collected Poems* (New York: Alfred A. Knopf, 2004).

"The Green Cup" is for Steven Craig. "Milkman" is in memory of Jim Cessna. "Tomatoes" is for John Beckman. "The Custodian" is for Kenny. "Weeping Angel" is for Michael Zito. "Going to Sleep" is for Josh. "Summertime" is for Hayes. "Men at Sixty" is for Steve Resnick. "Honor Flight" is for Kenny, again.